RedDrop
REBEL GIRLS
GROWING UP POWERFUL

THE PERIOD & PUBERTY EDITION

Copyright © 2023 by Rebel Girls, Inc.

Rebel Girls supports copyright. Copyright fuels creativity, encourages diverse voices, promotes free speech, and creates a vibrant culture. Thank you for buying an authorized edition of this book and for complying with copyright laws by not reproducing, scanning, or distributing any part of it in any form without permission. You are supporting indie creators as well as allowing Rebel Girls to publish books for Rebel Girls wherever they may be.

Good Night Stories for Rebel Girls and Rebel Girls are registered trademarks.

Good Night Stories for Rebel Girls and all other Rebel Girls titles are available for bulk purchase for sale promotions, premiums, fundraising, and educational needs. For details, write to sales@rebelgirls.com.

Rebel Girls, Inc.
421 Elm Ave.
Larkspur, CA 94939
www.rebelgirls.com

Author: Nona Willis Aronowitz
Illustrator: Caribay Marquina
Art director: Giulia Flamini
Graphic designer: Kristen Brittain
Editor: Jess Harriton
Panel of Experts: Alexandra Vaccaro M.A., L.A.C.; Aline Topjian; Beth Lucas; Nicole Sparks, M.D.
Special Thanks: Eliza Kirby, Grace Srinivasiah, Jes Wolfe, Sarah Parvis, and Marina Asenjo

First Edition: May 2023
10 9 8 7 6 5 4 3 2 1
ISBN: 979-8-88964-084-4

CONTENTS

Introduction 4
Let's Get Ready for Puberty 6
You'll Get Your Period 12
Taking Care of Your New Body 20
A Step-by-Step Shaving Guide 26
Buying Your First Bra 28
Hair Tips 31
Being In Awe of Your Body 33
Quick Ways to Feel Empowered! 38
Your Body is Your Own 40
Get Moving! 41
Feeding and Fueling Your Body 46
The All-Important Sleep! 52
Ask the Experts 55
About RedDrop 58
Growing Up Powerful 60
The Rebel Girls App 61
More from Rebel Girls 62
About Rebel Girls 64

INTRODUCTION

Welcome, readers!

We are so excited about this partnership with Rebel Girls. It has always been a dream for RedDrop to have a book that provides tweens and their grown-ups with information that prepares and empowers them. This book, *Growing Up Powerful: The Period & Puberty Edition*, a special condensed version of Rebel Girls' *Growing Up Powerful* by Nona Willis Aronowitz, does just that. The original *Growing Up Powerful* is a celebration of the joy and messiness of growing up. It's filled with helpful advice, fun quizzes, and Q&As with experts and girls around the world. This RedDrop edition focuses on the period and puberty sections of *Growing Up Powerful*.

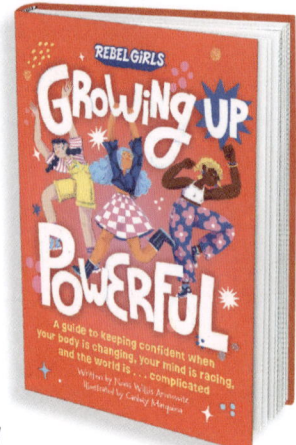

    RedDrop was co-founded by us, Dana and Monica. We are women of color and moms. Dana is an educator and Monica is a doctor. Over ten years ago when teaching a single-gender class of all girls, Dana realized there was a need for products that were sized for girls and for education that not only informs, but empowers. Years later, RedDrop was officially born.

    RedDrop is a service-oriented company that aims to serve every tween from the inside out. Meaning, every single thing our company produces in terms of products and educational materials is made to serve tweens and teens on their period and puberty journey. This is why we are so excited to partner with Rebel Girls to provide you with this fun, joyful, and informative book.

    We think it is super important to add here that we were raised by two empowering moms. Our moms intentionally drove us to be service oriented (our careers prove that!) and to be bold advocates for those in our care.

If you have never heard of RedDrop, that's okay—we are glad to welcome you! The RedDrop community started with our own daughters, Sterling, Kymani, and Mackenzie. Our girls tested our products and provided us with crucial feedback about the needs and wants of tweens and teens. It was their ability to use their voices that led us to continue to evolve and develop products, educational services, and a community free of stigmas and taboos.

RedDrop has served more than 55,000 tweens and teens. Working with Rebel Girls to provide you with this book is another way we get to serve our community. In these pages, you are going to learn all about the changes you'll experience during puberty, and how to love and care for your incredible, growing body.

Thank you for being here! Whether you are a mom, a caretaker, or a tween, having this book signifies that you are ready to empower yourself with knowledge, and we think that's awesome. We are so glad to welcome you!

In service,

Dana & Monica

RedDrop Founders

Dana & Monica

Download the Rebel Girls app to listen to meditations, exercises, stories from girls just like you, and conversations with our experts.

Whenever you come across a QR code, scan it, and you'll learn more about many of the topics in this book.

LET'S GET READY FOR PUBERTY

Part of growing up means going through the confusing, exciting stage called **puberty**. It could start as young as 8 years old or as late as 13—and the changes can happen in any order. Your emotions may be running wild and turning on a dime. But your body is going through a big shift too. So let's get into it.

Your Changing Shape

When you were a little girl, your body shape probably seemed similar to the boys around you. You had a flat chest and your waist might have been pretty much the same width as your hips. When a person assigned female at birth goes through puberty, the extra estrogen (the hormone that is responsible for developing female body parts) in her body often causes her hips to widen. You will probably gain some weight, but your waist may also become smaller compared to your hips. Regardless, you might see curves on your body that you didn't see before.

The reason for all these changes? It is so your body will be prepared to carry a baby one day, if you choose to have one.

Keep this in mind, though: there are all kinds of different body shapes. Not every girl's body will end up looking curvy, and not everyone's waist will get smaller compared to their hips. Some people are shaped like hourglasses, while others are shaped like sticks, apples, pears . . . you get the idea. Not only are all body shapes normal and healthy, but they are also usually determined by what our families look like, not what we eat or how we exercise. And remember, your body is going a little haywire right now. You probably won't know what your adult shape will be for many years. In the meantime, rest assured that your body is doing exactly what it's supposed to be doing: growing!

Your Breasts Will Make Their Appearance

One of the first and most noticeable parts of puberty is that your breasts will start to grow. This'll start to happen gradually, probably between the ages of about 8 and 13 (though a bit earlier or later is completely fine too). First, you'll notice what's called "breast buds"—little mounds under each nipple that may feel tender to the touch. Your nipples might get darker and bigger. As your breasts move through stages of growth, it's quite possible that they'll look pointy, lopsided, or a little wonky. Trust us: this is just part of a very natural process. By the time you reach the end of your teens, your breasts will settle into a more permanent shape—although one may always be a little different than the other, and that's okay too. There are infinite ways for breasts to look: round, teardrop-shaped, oblong, far apart, close together, big, small, firm, soft, and anything in between! All fine, fabulous, and unique to you.

Even if we tell you that all this is normal, it might still feel a little embarrassing to suddenly have these visible lumps under your shirt where you didn't before. And it can be equally nerve-racking if your breasts are taking their sweet time growing.

Puberty is a time when you may become self-conscious and start to compare your body to others, wondering if you, ahem, measure up. You may wonder if your breasts are "too small" or "too big." Despite what kids in school decide is fair game (and there are always a few gossips who think they can weigh in on your changing body), there isn't any such thing as "too" anything.

The fact is, each and every body is on its own time line, so the best we can do is accept what it has in store for us.

You Might Smell Different

Soon your body will be flooded with lots of hormones, which will (among other things) activate the sweat glands in your armpits. This means you'll start to sweat there more than before, and when that sweat mixes with bacteria . . . boom, you have body odor. This new stink is definitely funky—it can smell salty, onion-y, or even a bit like mac 'n' cheese. It's not always pleasant, but again (let's say it together): totally normal!

You May Get Your First Pimples

Those puberty hormones are little multitaskers. They are also busy affecting the oil glands in your body. Oil is essential for healthy hair and skin, but during puberty, it gets the message to produce like crazy. This extra oil tends to mingle with dead skin cells and bacteria. The result? You may notice some new, pesky pimples dotting your once-clear face, back, and chest. *Ugh!* There are few things more annoying than pimples (otherwise known as zits, officially known as acne). But they're often a part of life during this time and for a few years afterward. Most people have to deal with them at some point, even the people who appear to have flawless, glowing complexions. Pimples can show up in different forms:

Blackheads: These tiny, black dots can form when individual pores are clogged but still exposed to air. They're most common on what's called your "T-zone": your forehead, nose, and chin.

Whiteheads: These are also clogged pores, but they're white because they're closed, so the stuff inside of them doesn't go through the same darkening that happens when it is exposed to oxygen.

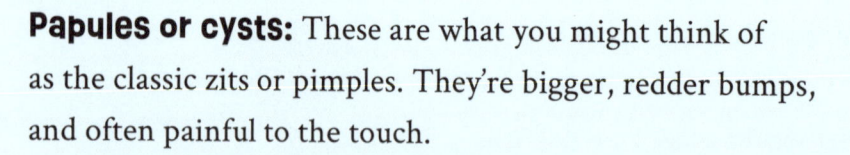

Papules or cysts: These are what you might think of as the classic zits or pimples. They're bigger, redder bumps, and often painful to the touch.

You'll Notice Hair in New Places

Your hormones are at it again. This time they're sending messages to your body to produce more hair. And not just anywhere. You'll start to notice some strands growing under your arms and between your legs. The hair that you see down there is called **pubic hair**. This hair might be light and soft at first, and then may get dark, coarse, and curly—although, much like the rest of our bodies, everyone's pubic hair texture and color are different. Your pubic hair might match the color of the hair on your head, or it might not. And like your breasts, pubic hair growth is usually a long, gradual process. It'll be years before you have the amount you'll have as an adult. Besides pubic hair, you might also notice that the hairs on your arms and legs are thicker too. The hair on your head might start to get oilier. Or not! We know we're starting to sound like a broken record, but everyone is different. So oily tresses or more hair in other spots on your body may be a big part of puberty for you . . . or you may not notice it at all.

You May See Some Goo in Your Underwear

Did you know your vagina cleans itself? It's true! During puberty, your vagina kicks into high gear and starts producing a clear or milky, mucus-like liquid called **vaginal discharge**. This stuff happens to everyone. It's your body making sure your vagina is clean, moisturized, and infection-free.

This discharge shouldn't smell like much. If it does, particularly if the smell is *bad*, tell a parent. This is a sign of possible infection, so you should head to the doctor.

YOU'LL GET YOUR PERIOD

At some point, after you've noticed some of the changes we've already talked about (and especially if you've noticed vaginal discharge), your body will reach a *big*, important milestone: you'll start bleeding from your vagina for a few days to a week every month. This is called **menstruation**, or, more casually, "getting your period." The average age for starting your period is around 12, though it might happen as early as 9 or 10, or as late as 14 or 15.

It may not exactly sound appealing. Blood? *From my vagina?* We'll admit, these few days aren't always the most comfortable or convenient. But while blood is usually a sign that we're hurt or that something is wrong, the beautiful thing about periods is that they're a signal of your body working exactly as it should. And it means that your body is gearing up to one day have a baby, when and if you're ready.

Okay, let's back up. Why exactly do we bleed every month? It all starts with your uterus, the place where your body would grow a fertilized egg that could eventually become a baby. All month, thanks to your hormones, your uterus will prepare for this possibility by lining its walls with blood. When there is no fertilized egg in the uterus (and therefore no fetus), the lining breaks down and flows through your vagina. That's it! That's your period.

Period blood doesn't look the same as the blood you see when you cut yourself or skin your knee—it can be darker and have more of a molasses-like texture, maybe with little clumps here and there. It might look more brown than red on light days. Your flow can be unpredictable at first, but it usually settles into a pattern eventually. A common cycle might start out with a heavier flow and then taper off after a few days.

What to Expect from Your First Period

The first time you bleed can look all kinds of ways, and it may or may not be the whole enchilada of a weeklong flow. It could be as simple as a smear of brownish red on your underwear. It could mean that you'll be having it monthly from now on, but more likely it'll take a while (sometimes a couple of years) for your periods to become regular. Many girls find that, after the first time, their periods disappear for a few months before they return.

So what if you go to the bathroom and see this telltale smear (or drip or gush)? Don't panic! You may feel a bit bashful or even ashamed, but there's no reason to be embarrassed. Some families openly celebrate this moment, and why shouldn't they? It's exciting! The menstrual cycle has enabled the birth of almost every single person on planet Earth. How cool is that?

Still, you're bleeding, so you do need to spring into action. If your period comes as a surprise, and you don't have any supplies with you, your first order of business should be to fold up a few squares of toilet paper and put them in your underwear to soak up the blood. Chances are you probably *won't* leak all the way to your outside clothes, but if you do, try to reach for the nearest jacket or sweater to tie around your waist. Then tell an older woman you trust that you've started your period. We guarantee that she'll recall exactly how this felt and help you find the things you need ASAP. Speaking of . . .

Tampons, Pads, and Other Products

One of the first issues you'll have to tackle when you get your period is how to catch the blood so it doesn't stain your clothes. The two most common options for dealing with the blood are pads and tampons. There's also absorbent period underwear, where you bleed right into the cloth—some even come in cute prints especially for girls your age. Those are better for the environment than pads, but they require a little cleaning effort. Finally, there are menstrual cups and menstrual discs, which are usually reusable and last longer than tampons. They take a while to get the hang of, though, so you may want to start with a more basic method.

Most girls wear pads at first, since they're the easiest to use. So let's talk about them. Pads are rectangle-shaped and made of thick, super-absorbent material. They come with a sticky side that goes directly onto your underwear, and some have "wings" that fold over the edges of your underwear to make extra-sure there aren't leaks. You'll need to peel off a thin layer of paper to expose the sticky side that adheres to your underwear. There are pads for all stages of your period, from the lightest to heaviest flow.

> **WHAT THE REBELS SAY**
>
> "We are all imperfectly beautiful, so let's embrace that."
> —Lili Reinhart, actor

Types of Pads

* Overnight (the thickest and most absorbent)
* Maxi (thick and very absorbent, for the absolute heaviest flow)
* Super (for continuous, still kinda heavy days)
* Regular (thinner, but they still soak up lots, for medium flow)
* Thin/Ultra Thin (for lighter flow days)
* Panty Liners (for trickles and spotting)

Pads come scented or unscented, and we recommend choosing unscented. Perfumes can irritate your sensitive parts and even cause infections—and there's really no need for them, anyway. As long as you change your pad frequently (every few hours or even less, depending on how much blood you see on it), you shouldn't have to worry about odor. When you're changing, be sure to tightly wrap the pad in some toilet paper and put it in the trash. No flushing!

What about tampons? They're definitely a bit more involved than just sticking a pad to your underpants. Tampons are tightly packed tubes of absorbent material that fit inside your vagina, often with the help of a cardboard or plastic applicator. They catch the blood before it reaches the outside of your body. The muscles in your vagina hold up the tampon, so don't worry—it won't fall out! Many girls love the convenience and comfort of tampons. When they're in right, you shouldn't feel them at all, and they make things like swimming and playing sports a lot easier during your period. But if you're not used to it, sticking something up there might seem scary or awkward, so take your time. Tampons will be there if and when you decide to use them.

When you do, set aside a little time in the bathroom to practice, practice, practice. Most girls find that a smaller-sized tampon (often called "slim" or "junior") is more comfortable at first. There are usually detailed instructions on the package about how to use the applicator and suggested positions to try in the bathroom in order to get the most comfortable fit. All tampons are a bit different, but here's a bit of info for the tampon newbie: there's a little bagel-shaped piece of tissue the size of a dime, called the "cervix," blocking the opening of the uterus, and the hole in the center is really tiny. So tampons can never, ever get lost inside you. That means the tampon is probably supposed to be in a little deeper than you might think!

Picture This:

Chloe was a week into her first summer at sleepaway camp when she woke up in the middle of the night feeling some cramping in her lower tummy. She headed to the bathroom with her flashlight. Sure enough, there was a streak of blood on her underwear. She'd gotten her first period.

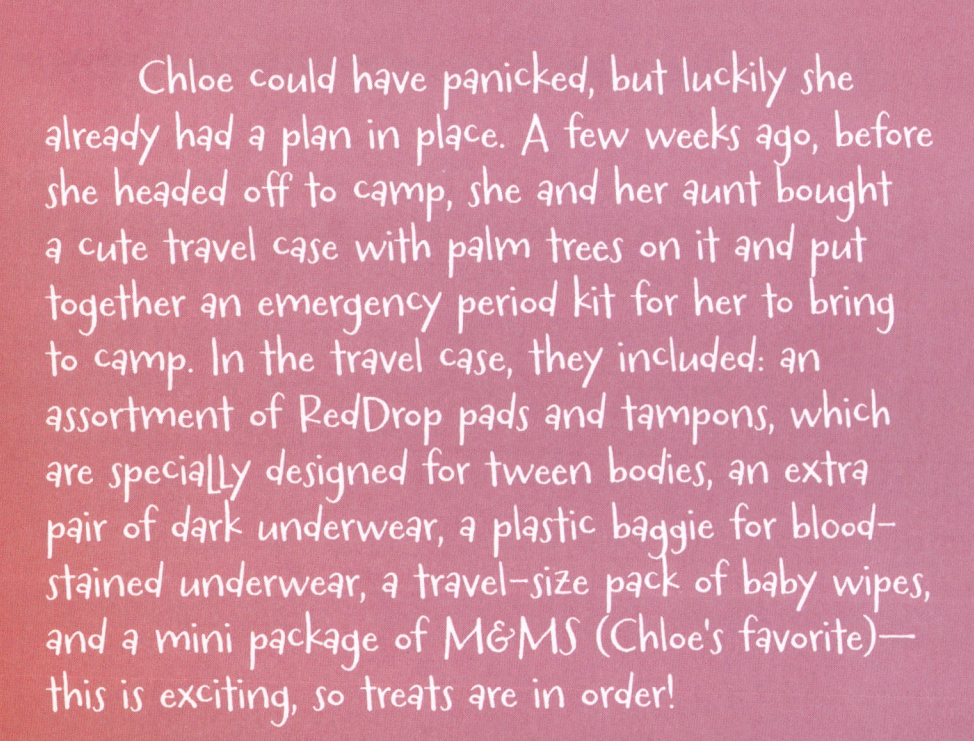

Chloe could have panicked, but luckily she already had a plan in place. A few weeks ago, before she headed off to camp, she and her aunt bought a cute travel case with palm trees on it and put together an emergency period kit for her to bring to camp. In the travel case, they included: an assortment of RedDrop pads and tampons, which are specially designed for tween bodies, an extra pair of dark underwear, a plastic baggie for blood-stained underwear, a travel-size pack of baby wipes, and a mini package of M&Ms (Chloe's favorite)—this is exciting, so treats are in order!

Chloe tiptoed back to her bunk and grabbed the toiletry case. In it, there was everything she needed—including a sweet surprise note that her aunt had slipped in at the last minute. Later that summer, when another girl in her bunk was caught by surprise by her period, Chloe knew just what to do. She slipped her one of the pads from the emergency kit.

One of the great things about getting your period—it's not only a major step of growing up, but it also inducts you into the "supply sisterhood" of being able to help out when another girl is in a jam!

What Your Period Might Feel Like

Listen, your period is incredible and nothing to be ashamed of, but it can also be a major pain. Sometimes literally. Period cramps are definitely a thing! It's hard to describe how they feel unless you've experienced them. They're usually more of a dull, constant ache than a sharp pain, but they can be intense. Not only that, but you may also feel more tired or sensitive during your period. That's why it's essential to come up with ways your body can feel comfier for that week or so.

Once you've had your period for a few months in a row, pay close attention to your particular flow. Take a warm bath or invest in a heating pad to soothe cramps. Build in time to take it easy and munch on your favorite treats. (Fun fact: the magnesium in chocolate actually might help your muscles relax!) Take a walk in the fresh air to energize you. If none of that helps, ask your grown-up about taking medicine, such as ibuprofen. And don't be afraid to speak to your grown-ups or doctor if you're in a *lot* of pain. Periods aren't fun, but pain that doesn't ease with mild painkillers could mean there's a more serious problem.

That Pesky Thing Called "PMS"

PMS—or "premenstrual syndrome"—is a collection of symptoms that might show up in the week or so before your period. (Once again, you can thank your hormones.) There are a ton of these symptoms, so here goes: you may feel bloated, tired, and headachy. You could feel constipated, or you could have a bit of diarrhea. Perhaps you'll crave sugar or salty foods. Your breasts or lower back might feel sore. You might notice more pimples than usual. You may also feel more emotional, anxious, weepy, or quick to anger during this time. The list goes on and on! Years ago, PMS symptoms weren't taken seriously by doctors, and there was even a myth that they didn't exist at all. Nowadays, though, it's generally accepted that PMS does exist, and even that there's a particularly intense form of it, called "premenstrual dysphoric disorder" (PMDD). Again, if any of these symptoms feel like they're a little too much or too intrusive in your life, don't be afraid to speak up.

TAKING CARE OF YOUR NEW BODY

Now you know all about the changes your body is about to go through. Not all of them are going to feel awesome, and some of them might require you to give your body a little extra TLC. Here's your road map to feeling and looking your freshest.

Protecting Your Skin

We talked about the different kinds of pimples you might be noticing on your face—all annoying, all here to ruin your day! Your first impulse might be to go on the offensive and buy every acne product in the skin-care aisle. This is exactly what you should *not* do. Mystery potions with lots of ingredients can cause skin to freak out and get even worse. An occasional face mask or yummy-smelling lotion is fine for fun, but the best thing you can do for your skin is wash it with a gentle cleanser and top it off with a few drops of an oil-free moisturizer. (Yes, even if you have oily skin—skipping moisturizer can tell your face to produce even more oil, worsening the problem.)

If your skin gets shiny throughout the day, it can be nice to reach for some oil-blotting sheets in your backpack. They're a quick and cheap way to freshen up.

Whatever you do, don't pick at or pop your pimples. It can leave scars or make a zit look worse. And it can hurt a lot!

There *are* a couple of products that can help mild acne. Look for creams with benzoyl peroxide (which kills bacteria) or toners with salicylic acid (which helps clean off dead skin cells). These drugstore products work best on mild or moderate breakouts. More serious acne is really the job for a doctor called a **dermatologist**. If you feel like your acne is getting in the way of you feeling confident and happy, talk to your grown-ups about making an appointment.

One more word about protecting your skin: you must, must, must use sunscreen! Chances are your grown-ups chased you around with a big sticky bottle of the stuff at the beach when you were smaller. Now it's your turn to take care of your own skin to prevent sunburn and skin cancer. (Not to mention wrinkles later on.) Sunscreen comes in all kinds of skin-friendly versions, like oil-free, face-sensitive, and spray-on. It's sometimes even included in face moisturizer, so you don't have to think about an extra step. It might be tough to think about a future you with sun damage, but take it from us: your skin will thank you later!

What About Makeup?

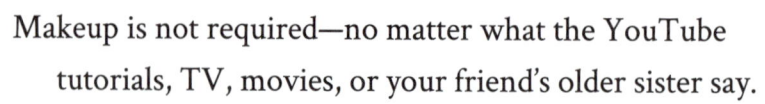

Makeup is not required—no matter what the YouTube tutorials, TV, movies, or your friend's older sister say. If you do decide to try it, remember that it's a way to have fun, accentuate your already gorgeous features, and express your creativity. It's not about "fixing" imperfections or keeping up with anyone at school. Think of makeup as a way to express your individuality, rather than to be like everyone else. And of course, if covering up that pimple on Picture Day will make you feel more confident, go for it! But remember, your face is 100 percent lovely just the way it is.

That said, makeup can be a blast to experiment with. It's up to you what look to go for (and, we're sorry to tell you, your parents might have a say in the matter), but our advice is to start slow. Try your hand at some tinted moisturizers, lip glosses, skin highlighters, and clear mascara. Big, bold colors might be too much too quickly, and foundation or powder might aggravate your sensitive skin. It also depends on where you are going. Things like glitter or electric-blue eyeliner might be fun for, say, sleepovers, but not school.

And finally, no matter how tired you feel, remember to wash your face and remove your makeup before bed!

Come Up Smelling Like Roses

Okay, obviously smelling like an actual flower all the time is impossible. But since puberty does mean we'll start to sweat more and therefore smell more too, you might want to start thinking about ways to freshen up. Step one: especially after your underarms start to have hair, take a few seconds to lather up those areas in the shower. Then, you could consider using a deodorant and/or an antiperspirant, which do different things (but are often combined into one product). **Deodorant** covers up the scent of body odor, either with other fragrances or with neutral fresheners like baking soda. **Antiperspirant** prevents or decreases how much you sweat by temporarily blocking the pores sweat comes out of.

Finding a deodorant that works for you might take some trial and error, especially when it comes to "your" scent. Also, it's not strictly required to wear deodorant at all, as long as you're making an effort to keep your pits clean.

Air It Out Down There

You might also start to sweat more between your legs than you used to (and, as we mentioned earlier, you could also notice some discharge in your underwear). Any moisture is heaven for bacteria and fungi that can cause stink or infections. So it's important to keep your crotch clean and dry too. Avoid putting soap *inside* your labia or vagina—it could upset the delicate balance of chemicals in that area—but be sure to suds up any pubic hair and the creases between your thighs and pelvis. Cotton underwear is the most breathable choice, so stick to that. And try to change out of your bathing suit in a timely fashion. Staying in wet clothes can cause rashes or an itchy, uncomfortable condition called a **yeast infection**.

Do I Need to Do Something About My Leg Hair?

Nope! You certainly don't need to remove your hair if you don't want to. It's becoming more and more common to go au naturel. But if you'd prefer to try a smooth look, there's no health-related reason why you shouldn't go ahead and try it. Just make sure to ask your grown-up first.

The most common way to remove the hair on your legs is to shave it. There's also waxing, which can be painful and expensive, and hair removal creams that dissolve the hair, which are pain-free but often smelly and not cheap, either. Let's focus on shaving for now, since it's the easiest method for a beginner. Here are some things to know.

> **Shaving is a commitment.** A couple of days after shaving, your legs will feel a bit coarse and prickly with what's called "stubble." It happens when hair is bluntly cut by a razor, and it means that you'll have to routinely shave in order to keep that silky feel. So make sure you're prepared to keep shaving, or at least have a week or two of the rough stuff on your legs.

Shaving isn't without its "ouch" moments. A razor can create irritated red bumps, called "razor burn," if it's not helped along with a sufficiently slippery goo like shaving cream or lotion. Also, when dragged the wrong way, it's possible to cut or nick yourself with a razor. So proceed with caution.

All razors are not created equal. There are disposable razors that you throw away after a few uses and permanent razors with blades you replace. There are single-blade razors and double-blade razors and even triple-blade razors. There are also razors that are marketed to girls, but they're really not all that different from the razors men use to shave their faces—besides maybe being a pretty color or a stylish shape.

Disposable razors are cheap, but replaceable razors are better for the environment. Whichever kind you choose, make sure the razors are new and sharp—or else you risk nicking yourself. Though their shave is not quite as close as double- or triple-blade razors, single-blade razors are probably best for beginners, since they're less likely to cut your legs.

A Step-by-Step Shaving Guide

1. **Get a bowl of warm water and a wet washcloth and bring them to an empty bathtub.** When you become a shaving master, you might be able to quickly shave in the shower. But for your first time, it helps to be on dry land.

2. **Wet your legs and apply a rich shaving cream, gel, or lotion.** Regular old hair conditioner works great too—anything that will coat your legs with moisture and will stay put during the shaving process. Some girls have noticeable hair only up to their knees so they coat only that part, while others will lather up their whole leg. It's up to you!

3. **Start at your ankle and work your way up.** The key here is to shave against your hair's natural growth pattern to get the closest shave. And remember to be as gentle as possible—pressing too hard can cause cuts and irritation.

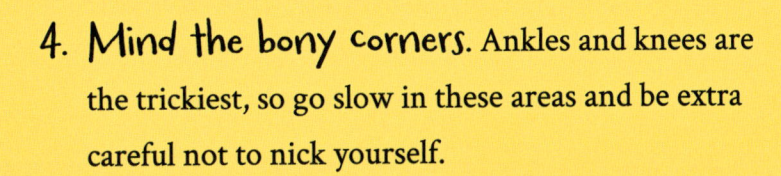

4. **Mind the bony corners.** Ankles and knees are the trickiest, so go slow in these areas and be extra careful not to nick yourself.

5. **Rinse out your razor in the bowl of warm water after one or two strokes.** Depending on how much hair you have, you may not have to clean the razor *every* time. But the less clogged it is, the better the results.

6. **When you're done, wash off your legs.** You can do this with the wet washcloth or the tub's spout, depending on how much extra shaving cream there is.

7. **Wait for the lotion!** Your skin might be a bit sensitive, so hold off on applying any lotion or oil for an hour or so after shaving.

And . . . you're done! Enjoy the silky smoothness.

Buying Your First Bra

If a bra sounds like something you want to try, talk it over with your grown-up first and discuss what bra you might like to get. This first shopping trip might be a little awkward, but it can also be kind of fun, in the way shopping for any clothes can be. Bras come in all kinds of shapes, sizes, and patterns. Some girls opt for a playful hot-pink or polka-dot bra, while others prefer to buy one in white or in a color closer to their skin tone so it's invisible under a shirt.

Here are some introductory bras you might consider on your very first shopping trip.

Tank tops and camisoles: While not technically bras, buying one of these could allow you to test out the feel of wearing something stretchy under your shirt without fully committing to Being a Bra-Wearer.

Training bras: These smaller bras are for girls who haven't started developing yet or are at the very beginning of their development. They're soft and stretchy and usually you just pull them over your head—no tricky clasps or anything. They don't really "train" your breasts for anything, but it could help *you* get used to the idea of wearing a bra. It all comes down to confidence and comfort. If a training bra will do that for you, go for it!

Sports bras and bralettes: These are stretchy, tight bras that feel a bit like tank tops, only they don't cover your stomach. Some of these have adjustable straps for a nice, snug fit, but they're generally made of one continuous piece of fabric—not many seams or hooks.

Once your breasts get a little bigger, you might think about getting measured. An ill-fitting bra is truly a tragic experience. Not only can it make your chest look lumpy and misshapen, but it can also be monumentally uncomfortable! Fitted bra sizes have both a letter and a number, like 34A or 36D. The letters represent your cup size. The cups are the parts that cover your breasts. A is smallest, and the cup sizes go up from there. The numbers represent inches, and they're the circumference of your rib cage right under your breasts (or your "band size").

Many stores have a special salesperson who will help you figure out your size. This might sound like the most mortifying thing on Earth—*a stranger measuring my breasts??*—but this person has seen it all. It only takes a couple minutes, and they'll be able to ensure you have a perfect fit. You can also measure at home if that's more your speed.

For your band size: Without wearing a bra or shirt, take a soft or cloth tape measure and wrap it around your back and under your breasts, where a bra would normally sit—not too tight and not too loose, exactly how you'd like the band of a bra to fit. If you get an even number, that's your band size. Round up if you get an odd number.

For your cup size: Wear a bra if you already have one, so that your breasts are in the place you want them to be. (If you don't have one, unadorned breasts are fine.) Take the same soft tape measure and wrap it around the fullest part of your chest, usually on top of the nipple. Then subtract your band size from this number. *Voilà!* The difference is your cup size. 0=AA, 1=A, 2=B, 3=C, and so on.

HAIR TIPS

Puberty can change the hair on your head without warning. A surge in estrogen can make your hair thicker and glossier, or the wavy hair you've had since you were a child can suddenly turn into tight curls. No matter what texture you have, it's yours and it's awesome. But now that you're largely caring for your own body (and since no one likes a bad hair day), it's worth taking a little time and getting to know what's good for your hair type.

In our experience, too many products can make hair look dull or oily. (And they can get expensive!) So, we found one secret weapon for your hair type that will keep your tresses looking fabulous.

Hair Type: Fine and Straight
Secret Weapon: Dry shampoo. It adds a nice texture to thin hair, and it can help dry out any excess oil between washings.

Hair Type: Thick and Straight
Secret Weapon: A few drops of oil or serum. Your hair can soak up just about anything, so just a little bit of gloss will make it look shiny and healthy.

Hair Type: Wavy
Secret Weapon: Sea-salt spray. A spritz or two of beachy salt spray can make waves look more defined.

Hair Type: Fine and Curly
Secret Weapon: Sulfate-free conditioner. It'll keep frizz to a minimum without weighing down your hair.

Hair Type: Coarse and Curly
Secret Weapon: Curl cream (or a spot of conditioner in a pinch). Your hair needs moisture, but it can also need some help staying bouncy. Curl cream does both!

Hair Type: Coily
Secret Weapon: Deep conditioner or hair mask. Tightly coiled hair can get dry easily, so invest in a rich, creamy conditioner and leave it on for 20 minutes before washing out.

BEING IN AWE OF YOUR BODY

Even though you might understand that all these body shifts are natural and expected, it can still be a struggle sometimes to accept this new skin you're in. It doesn't help that just as you're going through monumental changes, it seems that people at school and on the internet will have a lot of opinions about how thin or curvy to be, what clothes are in style, and what hairstyles are cutest.

The best advice we can give you to block out all this noise is this: focus on what your body can *do* instead of obsessing over what it looks like. Have you noticed that your times at track practice have gotten better after you sprouted a few inches? Take a second to thank those growing bones. Are you usually the person in your household to dodge that seasonal cold? Be proud of your immune system. Were you the person with the most resolve and endurance on that group hike you just took? It's a wonderful thing when your heart, lungs, and muscles rise to the occasion. Your body has been with you through thick and thin—be kind to it, rather than criticize it.

You may have heard messages like "every body is beautiful" or "love your body no matter what." These sentiments mean well, and of course it would be lovely to feel 100 percent positive about your body 100 percent of the time—and maybe you do! If that's the case, feel free to skip this section. That kind of confidence is amazing, inspiring, and deserves to be celebrated. But

> **WHAT THE REBELS SAY**
>
> "It doesn't really matter how you look in pictures. It just matters that you're there."
> —Megan Jayne Crabbe, body-positivity advocate

for some of us, feeling cool with our appearance all of the time isn't realistic. It's okay to get a little frustrated with your body or feel a bit awkward about its changes. For some people, something called **body neutrality** is more useful than body positivity. Body neutrality doesn't mandate constant love of our bodies so much as respect for how hard they work for us every single day. Besides, beauty isn't the most important thing in the world.

Your value shouldn't be tied to how you look.

Try to focus on things like your intelligence, your empathy, your sense of humor, your strength—not whether you're judged as beautiful by the outside world.

Picture This:

For as long as she could remember, Ellie was one of the shortest and thinnest girls in her class and on her swim team. But over the summer, she suddenly grew several inches and her once-lean frame now had curves where there weren't any before. Ellie didn't feel totally comfortable in this new body. She felt like people stared at her at the pool, and she had to get all new clothes.

But one day, Ellie started to appreciate her body in a completely new way. It all happened at her first big swim meet of the year. As she waited at the edge of the pool, crouched on her starting block, she felt her familiar self-consciousness. She adjusted her swimsuit for the thousandth time. It felt like all eyes were on her. But when the starting horn went off, she forgot all about her new insecurities. It was just her and the pool. She noticed that she was stronger than she thought—certainly stronger than she was last year, before her growth spurt. Her legs were pushing her faster, her arms were stretching farther, and her lungs were lasting longer without breaths.

When she reached the touchpad and brought her head up from the water to look at her time, she was stunned. She shaved a whole five seconds off her 100-meter freestyle! It was then that she realized those extra inches aren't so bad. After that incredible swim meet, she kept noticing more amazing changes. She could reach the high shelf in her kitchen. She could more easily lift her little sister. Pretty soon, she stopped wishing she could go back to her little-girl body. Instead, she started to really embrace and appreciate all the new things her body could do!

Evaluate What You See on TV and the Internet

No matter how committed you are to not thinking or talking negatively about your body, it can be hard in the face of the images we see every day on our phones and TV. The seemingly perfect bodies and faces of movie stars, influencers, and models can threaten to erase all the good stuff we know about our own regular bodies. These people are literally paid to spend lots of time on their looks and their bodies, sometimes in ways that are unhealthy. And many of the images we see of these professional beautiful people aren't even real—many of them have been edited using a program like Photoshop, where someone can take a picture of a person and whiten their teeth, make their legs or waist thinner . . . the list goes on. Actor Lili Reinhart has been outspoken about how social media can make us feel bad about ourselves. She has said, "Do not set impossible goals of meeting those fake standards. It's unrealistic to think that your body or my body will ever look like anyone else's. That's not the way it's supposed to be. We are all imperfectly beautiful."

There have been studies showing that social media can hurt teen girls' mental health. So if you're someone who uses Instagram, TikTok, or other platforms, it's important to take breaks from scrolling if you sense any negative emotions coming up. Remind yourself often that those images aren't real life. Support brands like Aerie and Dove that vow not to Photoshop the people in their advertisements. Feel free to immediately unfollow any accounts that make you feel down on yourself. Replace them with accounts that explicitly and joyfully celebrate the strength and power of the human body, such as body-positivity advocate Megan Jayne Crabbe.

How to Spot a Photoshopped Picture

One way to explode unrealistic expectations of yourself is to know when a photo has been edited up the wazoo. Examine the image carefully.

Signs an Image Has Been Edited

* Bent edges or liquidy-looking shapes
* Objects in the background that seem out of place or off
* Uneven color on someone's face or body
* Wildly out-of-proportion body parts
* Missing shadows or contours
* Impossibly creamy skin (everyone has pores!)

If you notice any of these things, then chances are the picture has been edited! Start thinking of these images as bizarre arts-and-crafts projects, not images with which to compare yourself. They simply do not reflect the reality of the human body.

Quick Ways to Feel Empowered!

Let's face it we all have some low moments here and there. When this happens, take a minute to be present with your body and comfort yourself. Here are a few ideas.

Body appreciation mantras: A mantra is a statement that you say or think that helps boost your confidence. Make a list of positive statements and set them aside for times when your confidence falters. An example of these might be:

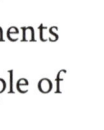

My body is unbelievably powerful.
My body knows just what to do, every minute of every day.
I'm growing and changing, and that's wonderful.

Giving thanks: Grab a pen and a piece of paper and literally thank your body for things it did for you today. This list could look something like this:

Thank you, reflexes, for protecting me from being burned on the stove today.

Thank you, nose, for sneezing out that dust this morning.

Thank you, tongue, for making it possible to taste that delicious smoothie after volleyball practice!

Power poses: Sometimes moving your body into a shape that gets your blood pumping and stretches your muscles can ground you in the moment and remind you of your strength. Examples of those could be:

Head high, feet wide, and hands on hips
Back arched, hands high and wide
One knee bent forward, two hands outstretched (like you're about to give a hug)

Text an empowerment buddy: Come up with a code word with your most positive, encouraging friend that basically means "I need a reminder of how strong and capable I am." The code word can be anything: something random like "macaroni" or something reassuring like "gut check."

Mindful Break

Scan the code to learn a calming and empowering relaxation technique.

Your Body Is Your Own

So now you know that it's a wonderful feeling to have the utmost respect for your body. Guess what? You can also insist that everybody else respects your body too—and your boundaries. Consent means that you get to decide what happens to your body and who gets to touch it. Yes, even your parents and the other adults in your life. When someone goes in for a hug and you're not feeling it, just say, "I'd prefer a high five today." If someone ever touches you in a way that doesn't feel good, you should feel free to say so. If you don't feel comfortable telling that person in the moment, let your grown-up know.

This also means, of course, that you need permission from your friends or anyone else if you want to touch them in any way. This doesn't always mean waiting for an explicit yes or no. It's also a good idea to be in tune with others' body language. If you notice a friend looking uncomfortable or backing away from your touch, take that as a sign that they probably don't want to be touched. When you meet someone, you can also straight-up ask them, "Do you do hugs or high fives?" It's a super easy way to find out what someone is comfortable with!

GET MOVING!

What comes to mind when someone says "exercise"? Is it a treadmill at the gym, a soccer game, swim lessons, weights, a stretchy yoga class, or a hike? The answer is, of course, all of the above! As long as your muscles are working and your heart is beating faster than normal, whatever you're doing counts as exercise, which is awesome. Even though it's not always that easy to motivate yourself, almost everyone can admit that *having done exercise* is a fabulous feeling.

Why wouldn't it be? Moving your body is all-around great for you. It strengthens your muscles, including that muscle in the middle of your chest: your heart. Somehow it gives you more energy *and* makes it easier to sleep at night. A win-win!

Not only is it good for your body, but it also works wonders for your mind. Getting your heart rate up increases blood flow to your brain and helps your brain grow new blood vessels. Exercising releases chemicals called **neurotrophins**, which improve your memory and learning ability. (You might wanna do a few jumping jacks between study sessions!)

And working out can be a lifesaver when your moods feel out of your control. When you exercise, your body is flooded with **endorphins**, which is your body's homegrown way of relieving stress and depression. It can be a way to let off some steam if you're angry, distract yourself if you're having obsessive thoughts, or feel good about your body's strength if you're feeling negatively about how you look. Exercise isn't a magic solution to all your problems, but it really can make you feel good about yourself in lots of ways.

Everyday Exercise

Look, relaxing is awesome. We don't blame you if you're not used to moving your body regularly and you're afraid to begin a routine. But you don't have to be on a sports team or have good coordination to go out and exercise. Don't worry—you can start small and low-key! Nobody has to train for a marathon, now or ever. Here are some simple ways to get your blood pumping.

Take a walk instead of asking for a ride. It's that simple! This is the most basic, natural way for humans to get around, and even though it might not *feel* like fitness, it most certainly is. You're working your leg and butt muscles just by walking. And if you walk briskly, your heart rate will creep up. Walking is a fantastic way to clear your head and get some sunshine on your face—but it's legitimate exercise too.

Or take a dog for a walk. Does walking seem a little . . . pointless? Take a dog! That will give your walk a purpose and a healthy pace—most dogs like to keep it moving. If you don't have a dog, offer to walk your busy neighbor's dog. They'll be happy they don't have to pay a dog walker.

Play with your own weight. You don't need any fancy equipment to put some resistance on your muscles. All you need is your own body. Find a rug or a towel and do a few squats, lunges, sit-ups, and push-ups. You can even do standing push-ups by pushing your arms against a wall. If that feels okay, do a few more. No pressure!

Bike around your neighborhood. Biking is a wonderful way to strengthen your leg muscles and get your heart rate up. It's also a lot of fun! Gliding down hills, feeling the wind in your hair and the sun on your face—what could be better? You can also get a group together and bike to the shops to grab a lemonade or refreshing drink after all your hard work.

> **WHAT THE REBELS SAY**
>
> "When I play soccer, I feel that every kick allows me to free myself of the negative things inside me."
> —María R., 12,
> Zapopan, Mexico

Learn a few yoga stretches. Yoga is a form of exercise that not only stretches and flexes your muscles, but can also help along mindfulness, body acceptance, and relaxation. There are lots of YouTube videos that will break down the basics of sun salutations for beginners.

Throw a dance party! Dancing is a great way to move your body because you can do it pretty much anywhere, either solo or in a group. Maybe you just want to play your favorite song in your bedroom and jump around. Or perhaps you and your bestie can learn that new dance that's been blowing up online!

WHAT THE REBELS SAY

"On the first day of basketball, I tried, and I didn't enjoy it at all. But I kept playing, and overall, I had fun playing with my friends."
—Ellie H., 10, California, USA

When You're Exercising, Don't Forget To . . .

Drink lots of water. Hydration is important when you're sweating and working your muscles.

Stretch before you go. Getting a cramp when you're on a roll is super annoying, so warm up first.

Listen to your body. If it feels like too much at any point, stop. If you're in pain, stop. If you're exhausted and out of breath but feel like you "should" keep going so you can reach your goal, you should probably stop. Exercise can be a challenge, but it shouldn't be a punishment.

FEEDING AND FUELING YOUR BODY

We hear a lot about "healthy foods," but not everyone—not even doctors—always agrees about what that is. The bottom line is that some foods, like candy or snacks, with lots of oil, fat, sugar, or salt, are packed with empty calories and don't really nourish your body. Others have what food scientists call "nutritional value"—they have lots of vitamins and minerals, or whole grains and proteins. But that doesn't necessarily mean you should *never* have empty calories or *only* have extremely nutritious foods. Let's look at a few basic truths that most people can agree on.

Eat lots of fruits and veggies. You can't have too many of these. Fruits and veggies are often loaded with vitamins you need to grow, as well as fiber, which helps your digestive system be more regular—that means going number two every day or almost every day.

Variety and moderation are key. Pretty much everything is fine to eat, as long as it's not the *only* thing you eat. And as a general rule, you should eat more nutritious things than non-nutritious things. For example, having a handful of berries is great, but a handful of cookies is probably not the best choice—stick to one or two. Eating a balanced diet will make sure you get all the nutrition you need, but it'll still allow you to enjoy a wide variety of foods. A simple rule of thumb is to have a colorful plate at every meal.

Give your body fuel throughout the day. Eating a good breakfast before school helps you stay alert during class. A big nutritious lunch helps you avoid a four o'clock slump. And a healthy dinner sets you up for a solid night's sleep. A couple of snacks mixed into your day is fine too. You're growing at a speedy rate, so you need to refuel!

Listen to when your body says "I'm hungry" and "I'm full." There's no hard-and-fast rule about how much to eat, so it's best to just go by your own stomach's cues. Pro tip: it takes about 20 minutes for your brain to register how much food is in your stomach. So if possible, having a leisurely meal is best.

Pay attention to what foods make your body feel good. What meals leave you the most energized? What makes you feel slow and tired? Does your tummy hurt after eating certain foods? Starting to tune into how you react to foods is key to a healthy body.

When Food and Exercise Take Over Your Brain

Being conscientious about your health and how your body feels is usually a good thing. However, sometimes people pay *too* much attention to diet and fitness—to the point where it starts to threaten their mental and physical health. While this is a time in your life when you need lots of healthy food to grow, it's also a time when you may start to be more conscious of how your body looks to others. Add in a culture that's obsessed with losing weight and looking "perfect," and our relationship to food and exercise can get pretty messed up. Which is such a shame because they are wonderful things on their own!

Here's the thing: diets that promise magic results and lots of weight loss are very, very unlikely to work. And they're often not healthy. So they end up being a waste of time. Why count calories when you could be reading a good book, going on a bike ride, or hanging out with your friends?

Right now, your body and brain need all the nutrients they can get! Rather than worrying about every morsel you eat, it's best to take care of your body as best you can and accept its little imperfections. The things you don't like about your body now, you might love in a few years—that happens all the time!

Eating Disorders and How to Spot Them

We can tell you not to obsess about weight until the cows come home, but we also know that, for some people, it's easier said than done. Sometimes, worries over food and exercise can become a full-blown eating disorder. Disorders like **anorexia** (which involves serious restriction of food and fear of gaining weight) or **bulimia** (which is when someone binges food and then throws it up) can negatively affect your heart, bones, teeth, digestive system, and more.

The good news is that eating disorders can be treated—but only if they're noticed. Not everyone who has an eating disorder is very thin or obvious about their behavior.

Here are a few questions to ask if you suspect that either you or someone you love has an eating disorder.

Do You or Does Your Loved One . . .

* skip meals?
* focus on and complain relentlessly about food, calories, portions, and exercise?
* seem to have lost a dramatic amount of weight in a short time?
* constantly say you/they feel or look fat?
* make excuses for not eating?
* eat in private or act secretive about food?
* seem to excessively exercise?
* often leave during or after a meal to use the bathroom?
* have rituals attached to meals, like chopping up food into tiny pieces?

If the answers to any of these questions are "yes," it may be a sign of disordered eating. It can be really, really hard to approach a friend whom you suspect might have an eating disorder. Often, secretiveness is a big part of it, and they may deny that anything is wrong. The best you can do is be nonjudgmental, tell them you're concerned and that you care about them. If their health seems in serious danger, though, you shouldn't feel bad about telling the grown-ups in your friend's life. Eating disorders can be easy to hide, and lots of people ignore them or downplay how harmful they are. So sometimes adults need that extra heads-up from people who know their kids well.

And if you're the one who might have an eating disorder, or is veering toward unhealthy habits? We realize this might be the hardest thing ever, but try to be honest with the people around you, as soon as possible. Mention how you're feeling to a parent, a school counselor, or even a friend to start. It's important to say something right away, even if you don't think you have an out-of-control disorder. It's much easier to treat this issue if it's caught early. There are doctors and therapists who are trained in these kinds of disorders who can help. There are also support groups where those who are struggling can talk to others with the same issues. You definitely don't have to go through this alone!

The All-Important Sleep!

As your kid body starts to transition to your adult body, one of the most helpful things you can do for it is get enough sleep. You probably already know that sleep restores your energy levels, but catching enough Zs also improves health in many, many other ways. Sleep prepares your brain to learn—that's why you should hit the hay early the night before a big test! Getting enough sleep is proven to boost your mood. It also makes it possible to think more clearly and prevents you from getting sick. Here are some tips for how to get good-quality sleep:

Stick to a routine. Head to bed at the same time every night. This will get your brain and body in the habit of knowing when it's time to fall into dreamland. Brush your teeth, wash your face, and try doing some gentle stretches to wind down.

Limit screentime before bed. The blue light from phones and tablets has been proven to keep you awake even after you've shut them down. A couple hours before bed, put away the devices and pull out the book you're reading or your sketchbook or journal for a calming evening activity.

Make your space comfy-cozy! Every night, slip into some soft PJs—breathable cotton ones are usually best—and fluff up your favorite pillow. Try to notice how your body feels during the night and plan accordingly. If you tend to kick off the blankets because you're too hot, turn on your fan before bed. If your feet always feel like ice pops, put on your fuzziest socks to keep them toasty warm.

Start a dream journal. This is one way to make sleeping a bit more fun. Sometimes our dreams are pretty nutty, and it can be interesting to look back on all the outrageous images your mind conjured up during the night. The trick is to write down what you remember about your dreams as soon you wake up—otherwise they tend to float away quickly. Keep your dream journal close to your bed and start scribbling first thing in the morning.

You Get Only One Body. Be Good to It!

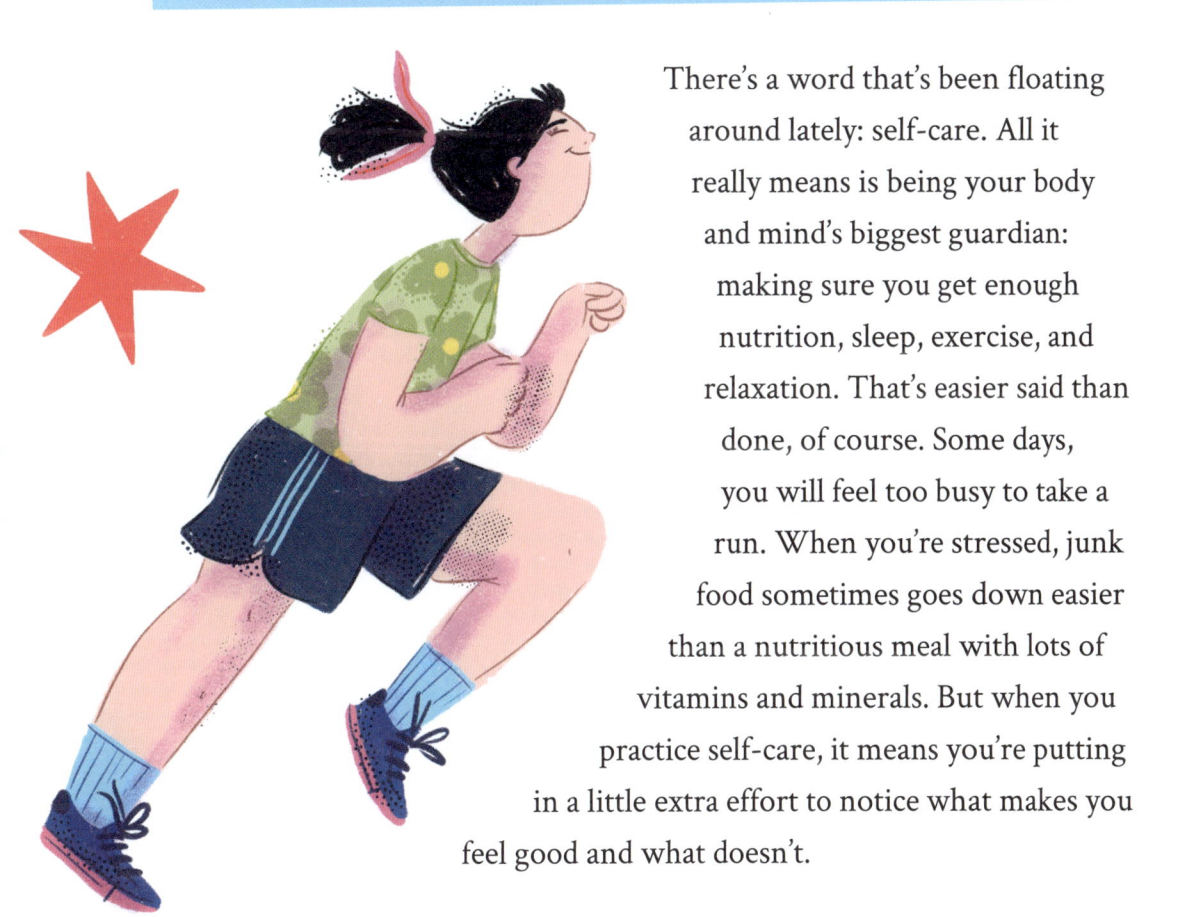

There's a word that's been floating around lately: self-care. All it really means is being your body and mind's biggest guardian: making sure you get enough nutrition, sleep, exercise, and relaxation. That's easier said than done, of course. Some days, you will feel too busy to take a run. When you're stressed, junk food sometimes goes down easier than a nutritious meal with lots of vitamins and minerals. But when you practice self-care, it means you're putting in a little extra effort to notice what makes you feel good and what doesn't.

If "self-care" sounds like one more thing you have to worry about and work hard at, remember this: *it actually feels good* to keep your body healthy and happy. Keeping it in good shape doesn't mean having the perfect physique or comparing yourself to other girls at school and actors you see on TV, or eating nutrient-dense foods 100 percent of the time. (Remember what we said about perfectionism? It's not worth it!) But taking care of yourself does mean tuning in to how your body feels on any given day. Sometimes saying no to certain things counts as self-care too.

In other words, if you're in the habit of looking out for yourself and your needs on a regular basis, you're already almost there. And by the way, having a sweet or salty treat is also part of self-care. It's your right—your job!—to give your body joy, not just discipline it.

ASK THE EXPERTS

When it comes to your changing body, lots of questions come up. Maybe you're wondering a bit more about things like periods, hormones, and body development. Well, we've got you covered! We sent questions from our readers to ob-gyn (obstetrician and gynecologist), Dr. Nicole Sparks.

> When exactly is my period going to happen?
> —Olivia R., 11, New York, USA

Your period will usually begin about two to three years after your breasts start to grow. This might happen around the age of 12 or 13. But don't worry if your period comes earlier or later than this. Some people can start their period as early as 9 or as late as 15. By age 15, most menstruating people (about 98 percent) will have had their periods. If you do not get a period by age 15, ask a parent to take you to a health care provider to assess.

Is it normal to feel emotional and not know why?
—Emma H., 9, Tennessee, USA

Yes, it is normal to feel emotional and not know why. There are lots of changes happening with hormones in your body leading up to and during your period. Your body is developing and so is your brain, so your emotions can be all over the place. You can be crying one minute and happy the next. You may be more sensitive or cry easier than usual on certain days. Here's what can help: get plenty of sunshine and sleep. Learn some breathing exercises which will help calm your body during those times where you feel emotional. And if some days, you want to cry, then cry! Letting it out helps too. Just know that it is normal to feel a wide range of emotions during this time.

> Does getting your period hurt?
> —Aliyah H., 10, Virginia, USA

Experiencing some pain right before or during your menstrual cycle is common. More than half of menstruating people will have pain from their periods for one or two days. The pain can feel like a bad cramp in your back or lower belly. Sometimes, you may also have nausea and diarrhea. The reason for pain during your period is because your uterus (the organ that holds a fetus), contracts and releases a chemical called prostaglandins.

You can use pain relievers such as ibuprofen one or two days before your period is supposed to start to alleviate any pain. Regular exercise, a warm bath, and heating pads also help relieve discomfort. If your period pain interferes with your daily activities or causes you to miss school, it is a good idea to seek help from an ob-gyn or another health care provider to make sure that everything is okay.

Let's Chat

Scan the code to listen to a conversation between our experts and girls just like you!

ABOUT

RedDrop

The mission of RedDrop is simple: We make products and educational materials for tweens, not grown-ups. Our products are created and sized for tween and teen girls as they start and continue along their period and puberty journey.

Our bestselling Period Kit offers a unique and empowering experience while providing quality products. Every single detail in our Period Kit promotes a positive period experience. The special little touches, like fun stickers and surprise gifts, come from our experience as girl moms—we know what girls love!

Here at RedDrop, we believe in the power of choice, and that is why we offer period products that allow girls to choose what is best for them. Our pads, period underwear, menstrual cups and tampons allow a tween and their grown-up to find the right product that will provide security and empowerment.

We simply exist to provide a positive period and puberty experience for tweens, teens, and their grown-ups—that's it and we love it.

You can find RedDrop products at www.tryreddrop.com and also on Amazon. We offer school and organizational pricing, as a big part of our mission is to ensure that every girl is prepared in the school environment. If you have any questions or need pricing, please email us at hello@reddrop.co.

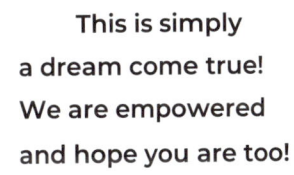

This is simply a dream come true! We are empowered and hope you are too!

Dana & Monica
RedDrop Founders

GROWING UP POWERFUL

All of the information in this special edition was pulled from the original Growing Up Powerful guidebook.

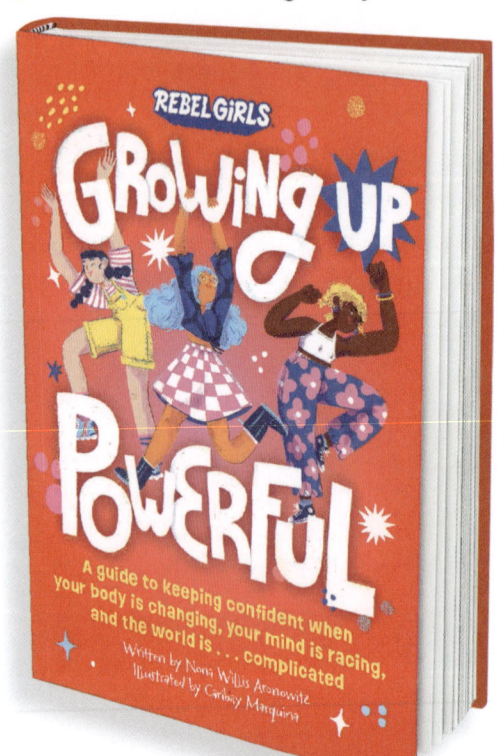

Filled with helpful advice, fun quizzes, and Q&As between experts and girls around the world, Growing Up Powerful is a bold, big-hearted guide to girlhood that will have teens and tweens feeling excited and confident about growing up.

Growing Up Powerful is available now, wherever books are sold. Scan the code to purchase your copy!

REBEL GIRLS APP

Listen to empowering stories on the Rebel Girls app.

You'll find exciting tales of extraordinary women from around the world. Scan the code to start listening!

Plus, for more confidence-boosting content, don't miss the Growing Up Powerful Podcast, available on the Rebel Girls app or wherever you listen to podcasts.

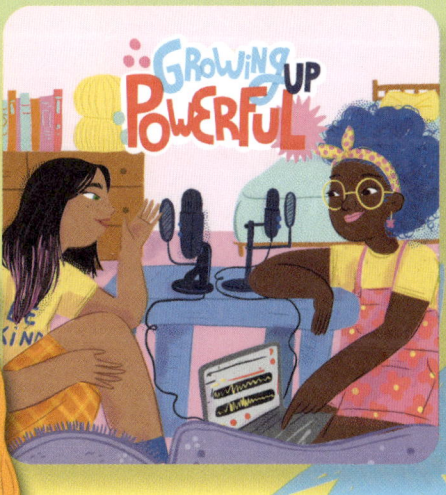

MORE FROM REBEL GIRLS

Let the stories of real-life women entertain and inspire you. Each volume in the Good Night Stories series includes 100 tales of extraordinary women.

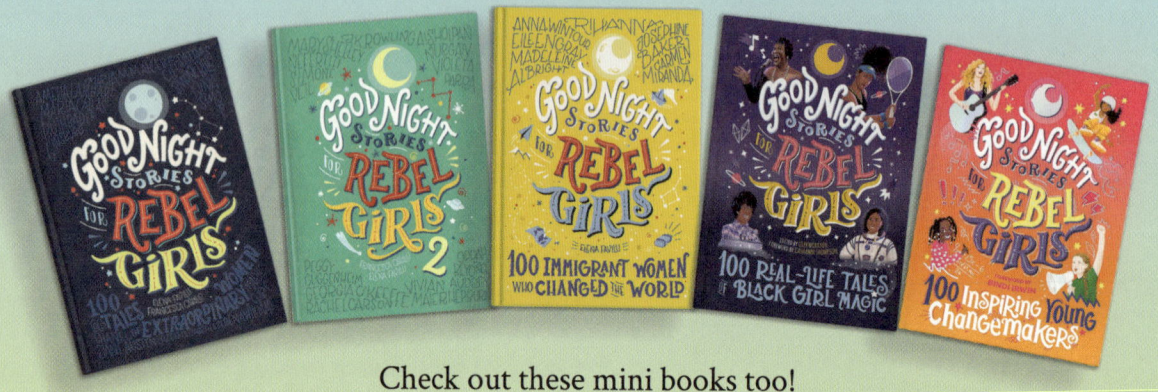

Check out these mini books too! Each one contains 25 tales of talented women, along with engaging activities.

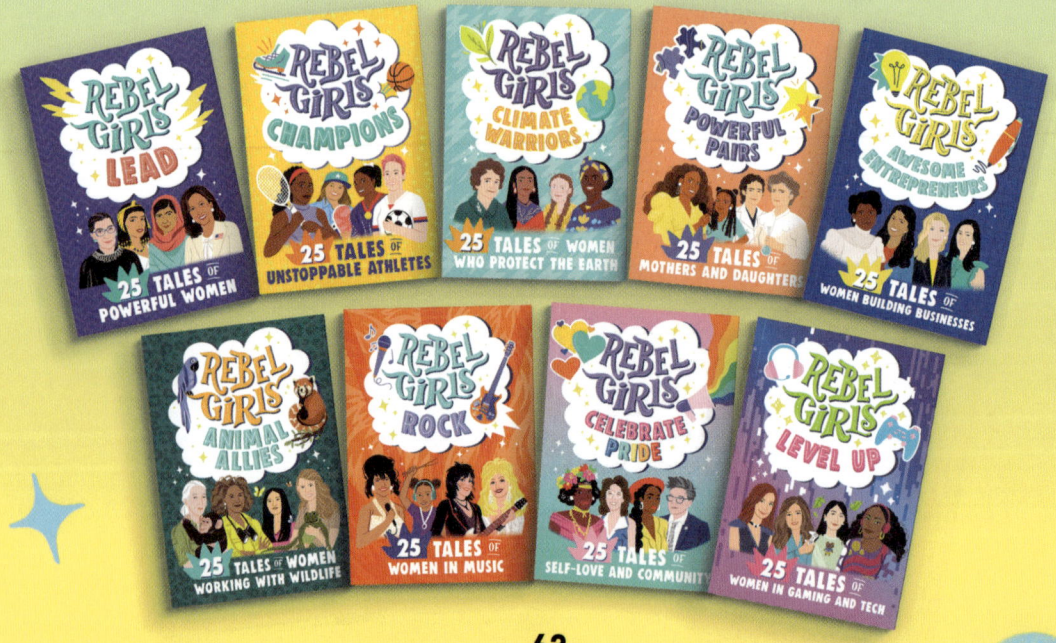

62

The quirky questions in these books help curious readers explore their personalities, forecast their futures, and find common ground with extraordinary women who've come before them.

In *Dear Rebel,* more than 125 extraordinary teens and women share their advice, experiences, and the secrets of their success—in their own words.

Dig deeper into the lives of these five real-life heroines with the Rebel Girls chapter book series.

Uncover the groundbreaking inventions of Ada Lovelace, one of the world's first computer programmers.

Learn the exciting business of Madam C.J. Walker, the hair care industry pioneer and first female self-made millionaire in the US.

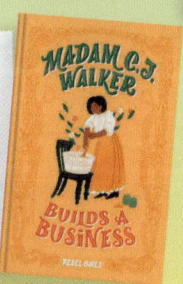

Explore the thrilling adventures of Junko Tabei, the first female climber to summit Mount Everest.

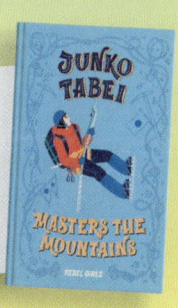

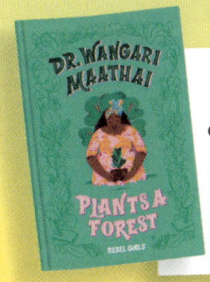

Discover the inspiring story of Dr. Wangari Maathai, the Nobel Peace Prize–winning environmental activist from Kenya.

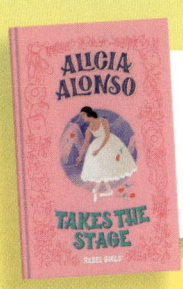

Follow the awe-inspiring career of Alicia Alonso, a world-renowned prima ballerina from Cuba.

ABOUT REBEL GIRLS

REBEL GIRLS is a global, multi-platform empowerment brand dedicated to helping raise the most inspired and confident generation of girls through content, experiences, products, and community. Originating from an international best-selling children's book, Rebel Girls amplifies stories of real-life women throughout history, geography, and field of excellence. With a growing community of nearly 23 million self-identified Rebel Girls spanning more than 100 countries, the brand engages with Generation Alpha through its book series, award-winning podcast, events, and merchandise. With the 2021 launch of the Rebel Girls app, the company has created a flagship destination for girls to explore a wondrous world filled with inspiring true stories of extraordinary women.

As a B Corp, we're part of a global community of businesses that meet high standards of social and environmental impact.

Join the Rebel Girls community:
- Facebook: facebook.com/rebelgirls
- Instagram: @rebelgirls
- Twitter: @rebelgirlsbook
- TikTok: @rebelgirlsbook
- Web: rebelgirls.com
- Podcast: rebelgirls.com/podcast
- App: rebelgirls.com/app

If you liked this book, please take a moment to review it wherever you prefer!